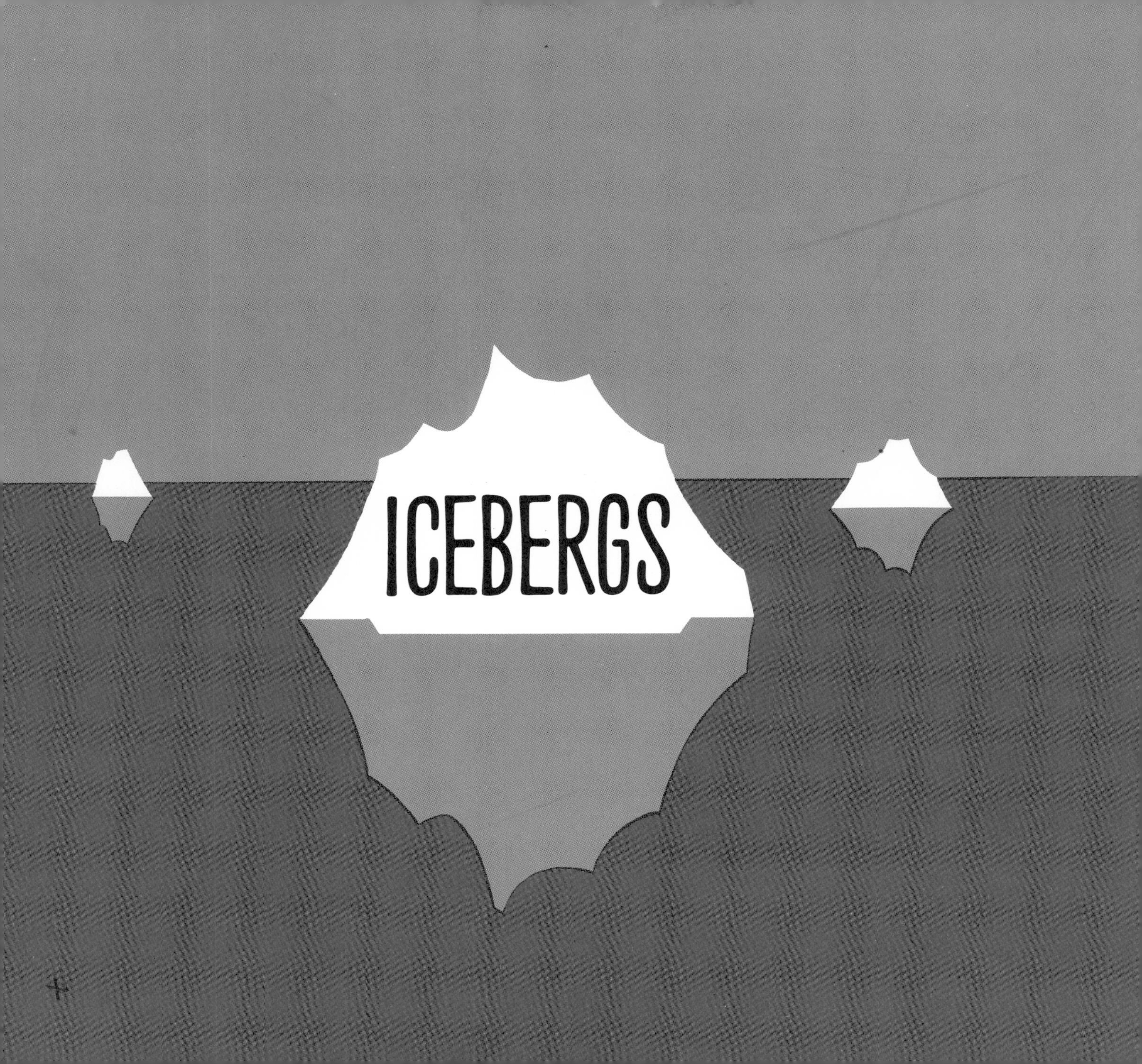
ICEBERGS

ICEBERGS

BY ROMA GANS

ILLUSTRATED BY BOBRI

THOMAS Y. CROWELL COMPANY   NEW YORK

LET'S-READ-AND-FIND-OUT BOOKS

Special Adviser: *DR. ROMA GANS*, Professor Emeritus of Childhood Education, Teachers College, Columbia University.

Editor: *DR. FRANKLYN M. BRANLEY*, Coordinator of Educational Services, American Museum–Hayden Planetarium, consultant on science in elementary education.

4   5   6   7   8   9   10

ICEBERGS

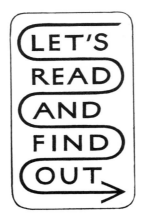

LET'S READ AND FIND OUT

Crack, crash, rumble, and roar.

An iceberg breaks from a glacier and moves into the sea.

It is a large and glistening mountain of ice.

It looks like a huge, sparkling castle.

It is an island made of ice moving into the sea.

Once this iceberg was part of a glacier.

Icebergs break from glaciers that form in the far north and the far south.

Glaciers are made of snow that has fallen for
   hundreds and thousands of years.
The snow that falls near the North and South Poles
   piles deeper and deeper through the years.

The snow packs hard and becomes ice.
 Now it is a glacier.
Ice in glaciers may be thousands of feet thick.
At the South Pole the ice may be three miles thick!
The glaciers made of this ice move slowly toward the
 ocean.

When a glacier reaches the ocean, waves beat hard
  against it.
Water pushes upward.
It makes deep cracks in the glacier.
With a loud roar a chunk of the glacier breaks off.
This great mountain of ice is an iceberg.
It makes large waves as it crashes into the sea.

The iceberg floats away from the glacier, farther and
  farther into open water.
The iceberg sparkles in the sun.
The colors change from blue to green or white like
  chalk.

Some icebergs are a mile long.
Some are so large that a whole city could be built on
them.
Some have peaks two hundred feet high, higher than
most buildings.

Most of an iceberg is below the water and cannot be
   seen.
There may be eight or nine times as much ice below
   the water as there is above.
The part below is much wider than the part above.
It is not round and smooth.
The iceberg has big, jagged edges.

Some icebergs move into parts of the ocean where
    ships travel.
If the iceberg is hidden by fog, a ship may crash
    into it.
Some ships have sunk after crashing into icebergs.
Captains steer their ships away from icebergs lest
    they strike the sharp edges hidden below water.

As icebergs move away from the cold seas in the far north and the far south they get into warmer water. Warm air is around them. The icebergs begin to melt.

Lakes and pools form in the hollows of melting
   icebergs.
The water looks blue and green and gold to the men
   who fly over icebergs.
Birds on long flights rest on icebergs and drink from
   the fresh water in the pools.
Icebergs give off fresh water because they are made
   of snow.
The ocean is made of salt water, which the birds
   cannot drink.

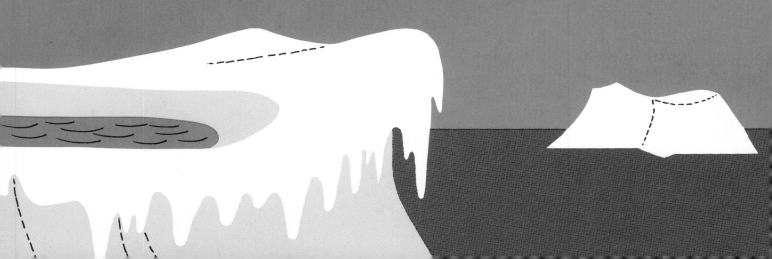

As icebergs float farther and farther into warm
weather they melt faster and faster.
Waterfalls rush down their slopes and spill into the
ocean.

Sometimes an iceberg tilts to one side.
It may even turn upside down.
Icebergs make big waves when they turn.

Large pieces of ice break from icebergs. They float away like little icebergs.

The coast guard sends men in airplanes, boats, and
helicopters to look for icebergs.
When icebergs are near a ship's path, the coast
guard sends a message to the ship's captain. They
tell the captain how big the icebergs are and in
which direction they are moving.
The captain steers his ship away from the icebergs.

After weeks and sometimes months an iceberg gets
so small that only a little part can be seen above
the water.

At last the sparkling island of ice melts away. It
disappears into the sea.

For hundreds and thousands of years snow has been
falling around the North and South Poles.
The snow packs and becomes ice.
The ice becomes a glacier.

The glacier moves slowly, slowly toward the ocean.
Crack, crash, rumble, and roar.
Another iceberg breaks off and moves into the sea.

ABOUT THE AUTHOR

Roma Gans has called children "enlightened, excited citizens." She believes in the fundamental theory that children are eager to learn and will whet their own intellectual curiosity if they are encouraged and provided with stimulating teachers and materials.

Dr. Gans received her B.S., M.A., and Ph.D. at Teachers College, Columbia University. She began her work in the educational field in the public schools of the Middle West as a teacher, supervisor, and then superintendent of schools. She is Professor Emeritus of Childhood Education at Teachers College, Columbia University, and lectures extensively throughout this country and Canada.

Dr. Gans is vitally interested in nature and all its phenomena. She has many bird-feeding stations at her house in West Redding, Connecticut, where she watches birds and their habits. She enjoys living in the country where she can observe the changing seasons of the year.

ABOUT THE ILLUSTRATOR

Vladimir Bobri is equally at home — and equally well known — in the fields of music and art. He is president of the Society of the Classical Guitar, editor of *Guitar Review* magazine, and an acknowledged authority on gypsy music.

Mr. Bobri was born in the Ukraine, where he attended the Kharkov Imperial Art School. He earned the money to come to this country in 1921 by designing sets and costumes for the Ballet Russe of Constantinople. Mr. Bobri has received a number of awards for children's book illustration as well as many citations from the Art Directors Club for his advertising design.